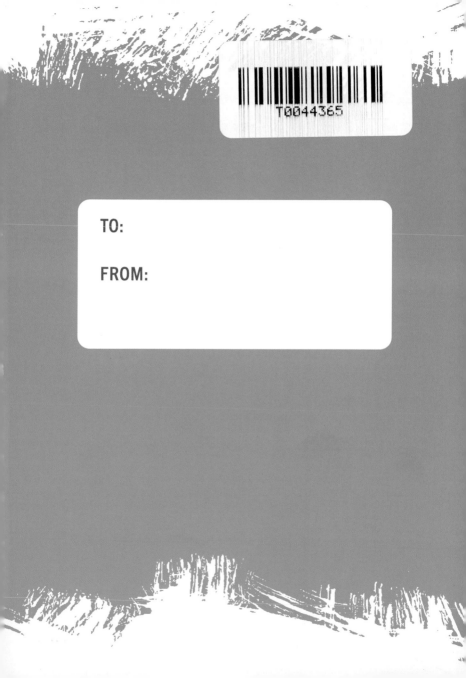

TO:

FROM:

THE

SIX-WORD

SECRET

TO

SUCCESS

EARL NIGHTINGALE

IGNITE READS
spark impact in just one hour

simple truths®
▶ Small books. BIG IMPACT.

For Diana—as the Earth thanks the Sun

CONTENTS

INTRODUCTION

In order to fully enjoy prosperity and its accompanying sense of achievement, one needs to have known poverty and an environment in which daily survival is the purpose of life. As a youngster, I didn't know anything about a sense of achievement, but I was all too aware of being poor. It didn't seem to bother the other kids, but it bothered me. What made it all the more exasperating to me, as a boy of twelve, was to be poor in Southern California, where there seemed to be so many who were rich. In fact, anyone who had an automobile, an electric refrigerator, and wall-to-wall carpeting was rich in my book, and the children of such people seemed to me to be fortunate indeed. I decided to find out why some people were rich while so very many of us were poor.

The year was 1933—the bottom of the Great Depression. Millions were unemployed. My two brothers and I were fortunate; although our father had disappeared in search of greener pastures, our mother never missed a day at her Works Progress Administration (WPA) sewing factory job. Her earnings, as I recall, were fifty-five dollars a month, which produced survival. We lived in "Tent City" behind the old Mariner Apartments on the waterfront in Long Beach, California.

"What makes the difference?" I asked myself. "Why are some people well off financially and others poor? Why are some so well paid while others are so poorly paid? What's the difference? What's going on here?"

I tried asking the adults who lived in our

neighborhood and soon discovered they didn't know any more than I did. In fact, I made what was to me an astonishing discovery: *The adults in our neighborhood didn't know anything at all.* They were pitifully uneducated—driven by instinct, other-directed.

My mother had many endearing qualities. One was her unfailing good cheer; another was her love of books. She haunted the public library, and my fondest memory of her is of her eating oatmeal and milk early in the morning under a dangling, naked, underpowered light bulb with a book propped up in front of her. She loved travel books, especially. Never able to travel herself, she explored the earth from pole to pole through her books on travel and adventure. I'm sure it helped save her sanity during those hard years. She was an attractive woman, still young but completely dedicated to the raising of her boys. Her books and our battered radio were her only entertainment. She read on her long Pacific Electric train rides to and from work in Los Angeles as well as after we boys had gone to bed at night. On weekends, after cleaning and doing the laundry, her books again filled her world with exciting travel and high adventure. Later in life, I realized she never had to stand in a sweltering customs shed, or see her luggage disappear into three Italian taxis, or struggle with a foreign language or currency, yet she had traveled from one end of the earth to the other and was intimate with the most remote places on the planet. That she was able to do so without ever leaving Los Angeles County was a tribute to the excellent public library system. It didn't cost her a dime.

And so it was to the Long Beach Public Library that I went seeking the elusive secret of success. I didn't know where to look among thousands of titles, but I felt sure the secret was there somewhere. It seemed to me that if anyone had ever figured it out, he or she would surely have written a book about it. After I began my search, I soon found myself sidetracked into the world of the most exciting fiction: the Hardy Boys, the great mind-expanding stories of Edgar Rice

Burroughs, and the Westerns of Zane Grey. Then came the fascinating stories of the Plains Indians by Stanley Vestal, and before I knew it I was as addicted to books as my mother. I learned about the importance of honesty, personal integrity, and courage and of believing in what is right and being willing to fight for it. I know that it was my early love affair with books that resulted in my getting a better-than-average education.

Later, as World War II loomed on the horizon, I left school and enlisted in the United States Marine Corps. However, I continued my studies—I read everything I could lay my hands on.

I made two decisions that guided the remainder of my life. The first was to discover the secret of success. The second was to become a writer. I loved books and wanted to write them myself. Toward the end of the war, I found myself back in the States working as an instructor at Camp Lejeune in North Carolina. Driving between the base and nearby Jacksonville, I noticed a radio station under construction. I decided to apply

for an announcing job, working nights and weekends. I auditioned and was hired. Sitting before the microphone at that small radio station, WJNC Jacksonville, North Carolina, was the beginning of my radio career. The owner-manager, Lester Gould, and I became good friends.

I took to broadcasting like nothing before in my life. I was in my element, and more than forty years later, I'm still in it. But my desire to write did not lessen, and gradually I began planning for the day when I would write my own programs. In the meantime, I learned the business, doing commercials, news, and station breaks. It was extra income and would prove to be valuable experience after I was mustered out of the Marine Corps.

My reading and search for the secret of success continued without letup, I studied the world's great religions. I found myself especially fascinated with philosophy and psychology. But it wasn't until one weekend when I was twenty-nine and working for CBS in

Chicago that enlightenment came. While reading, it suddenly dawned upon me that I had been reading the same truth over and over again for many years. I had read it in the New Testament, in the sayings of Buddha, in the writings of Lao Tse, in the works of Emerson. And all of a sudden, there they were, the words, in the proper order that I had been looking for, for seventeen years. The astonishing truth that *we become what we think about.*

It was as if I were suddenly immersed in a bright light. *Of course!* I remember sitting bolt upright at the thought of the simplicity of it. That was what Ortega was talking about when he reminded us that we are the only creatures on earth born into a natural state of disorientation with our world. It had to be because we are the only creatures with the godlike power to create our own worlds. And we do. We do create our own worlds all the years of our lives. *We become what we think about* most of the time. And if we don't think at all—which seemed to have been the principal problem of the people back in my old Long Beach neighborhood—we don't become anything at all.

There it was—just six words. There are more than six hundred thousand words in the English language, but those were the six I had searched for, in that particular order, ever since the age of twelve. Seventeen years it had taken to see the obvious. How could we become anything else? Our minds are the steering mechanisms of our lives. And each of us who does much thinking at all thinks differently. There at last was the secret of success or failure or something in between. Each of us is sentenced to become what he or she thinks about. Our brains are what make us human. How we use them decides our destiny.

1.

A RIVER OR A GOAL

There are two categories of very successful people: Those I call "River People" and those that might be labeled "Goal People."

River People are those fortunate few who find themselves born to perform a specific task. They are usually well aware of just what that task is while they are still quite young. They are not interested in doing anything else. They are born to spend their lives in great rivers of the most absorbing interest, and they throw themselves into those rivers wholly. Mozart and Leonardo da Vinci were River People. There are hundreds of thousands of River People living today, and they can be found in all fields. They are our finest musicians and performers in all the arts; they are writers, scientists, and lawmakers and can be found in every profession.

Dr. Al Rhoton, a brilliant microneurosurgeon at the University of Florida, comes to mind as I write on this subject. He heads the Teaching Center and performs brilliant, life-saving surgical procedures. I saw a dozen or so physicians from all over the world at the Center, sitting in a circle, peering through powerful microscopes and operating on the brains of mice in order to perfect their skills in microneurosurgery. They use instruments specially designed for such fine work—tiny, delicate forceps; sutures so fine they're nearly invisible to the naked eye; and miniature scalpels. Their movements are barely perceptible as they work on nerves and tiny blood vessels.

Dr. Rhoton can be seen in the halls of the hospital from early in the morning until very late at night. One sunny afternoon we were taking a walk, and I asked him why he didn't have a high-priced practice in New York or Beverly Hills. He walked along in silence for a few minutes, then he said, "Where I get my satisfaction out of all this, Earl, is knowing that somewhere in the world, every day, people are getting better medicine, better surgery, because of what we're doing here." His work is his life, and vice versa. I'm afraid his family has not seen too much of him over the years; that's true of all River People.

Henry Royce was such a person. His obsession was to build the world's finest and quietest motorcar. Early in the twentieth century, when he started work on what was to become the world's standard for excellence in automotive design and manufacture, the automobile engine sounded like a modern clothes dryer filled with empty cans, punctuated with gunshots. Royce was convinced that the parts of an internal combustion engine

3

could be finely manufactured to such exacting toler-
ances and so perfectly lubricated that the noise of their
operation would be (or could be) barely perceptible
to people standing nearby. He stalked about his auto
plant in a nearly constant march. He would not take the
time to eat—a boy was hired to follow him about with
a sandwich and a glass of milk. When Royce became
sleepy, he would lie on a cot in the plant and take a nap.
Then he was up again, examining everything.

One day he overheard one of his engineers saying
to a workman, "That's good enough," and Royce hit
the ceiling.

**"It is not good enough!" he shouted. "It is never
good enough. We strive for perfection. Since that's
impossible, it's never good enough. Find a way to
make it better."**

I once toured the Rolls-Royce plant in London and
was astonished at the care taken with imperfections
that were invisible to me. Such care and dedication put
England in good position during the Battle of Britain,

when Rolls-Royce turned out engines for Supermarine Spitfire fighters. A stained glass window over the entrance to the company's headquarters was given to the company by a grateful nation.

Royce's unrelenting dedication is typical of the River Person—the great products and services of the world are usually due to such a person. Henry Ford accepted the challenge—which was at the time thought to be impossible—to produce a motorcar for the working class. Ford did not invent the assembly line—Eli Whitney had done that with the manufacturing of rifles—but Ford was the first to apply the system to the manufacturing of automobiles. His genius for finding ways to cut costs and still produce a quality product was legendary. He raised the salaries of workers to a mind-boggling five dollars a day—a level never before equaled in the history of the Industrial Revolution. One of Ford's problems was that once he came up with a revolutionary idea, he was irrevocably fixed on it. The passage of time and changing economic conditions could not bring about changes in his way of thinking. But Henry Ford was a River Person. I'm sure you can think of many others. Perhaps you are a River Person.

Things aren't as simple and clear-cut as they once were. There's such a welter of possibilities—so many options—that it can be difficult for a person to find his or her main interest in life. If we haven't found the work for which we're best fitted, there is usually an unresolved feeling of discontent with what we are doing. If we were true to ourselves, we would say, *I know this work is not the work for which I'm designed*, and begin to explore, in our spare time, other lines of endeavor. Too often we are guided more by the pay scale than by a genuine feeling of interest in the work itself. Whatever our true line of work turns out to be—with the kind of 100 percent dedication and commitment we would give to it—it could produce everything we could possibly want.

Audio publishing did not exist as a business before

we started our company, and we became the world's leader in positive audio programs. It can still be necessary, as it was for us and for Steve Wozniak and Steve Jobs of Apple, to have to start something new. Our company began with my writing and recording *The Strangest Secret*. Perhaps there's some pioneering work for you to do too.

The old motion pictures keep coming back on cable television. Recently I caught a glimpse of a film that starred Mickey Rooney when he was a boy of perhaps thirteen or fourteen. Even before that, he had been a seasoned vaudeville and motion picture veteran. He was a natural, as they say. He took to show business the way Mozart took to music or Edison to tinkering or Lindbergh to flying. Today, Mr. Rooney is a distinguished actor with an ability to do comedy, tragedy, or musicals with equal facility. He has been a show-business phenomenon since childhood. Success is something Mr. Rooney didn't have to worry about. He has a great, deep river of interest that has entertained millions and will go on entertaining millions for many years to come.

Walt Disney was another good example of a River Person; so were Birdseye of frozen food and Hershey of chocolate. River People are perhaps the world's most fortunate people; they identify the star they are meant to follow, and they follow it all their lives.

Each of us should watch for early, telltale signs of consistent and unusual interest, for the magnet in the midst of the spectrum of options that draws us toward itself as light is drawn toward a black hole. On rainy days, when you were a child, out of school, what did you most enjoy doing?

Dr. Abraham Maslow has pointed out that in the best instances, the person and the job fit together like a key and a lock, or perhaps resonate together like a sung note that sets a particular string in a piano into sympathetic resonance.

He also said,

I have found it most useful for myself to differentiate between the realm of being (B-realm) and the realm of deficiencies (D-realm)—that is, between the eternal and the practical. Simply as a matter of the strategy and tactics of living well and fully and of choosing one's life instead of having it determined for us, this is a help. It is so easy to forget ultimates in the rush and hurry of daily life, especially for young people. So often we are merely responders, so to speak, simply reacting to stimuli, to rewards and punishments, to emergencies, to pains and fears, to demands of other people, to superficialities. It takes a specific, conscious effort, at least at first, to turn one's attention to intrinsic things and values— perhaps seeking actual physical aloneness, perhaps exposing oneself to great music, to good people, to natural beauty, and so on. Only after practice do these strategies become easy and automatic so that one can be living in the B-realm.

I believe that each of us, because of the way our genetic heritage is stacked, has an area of great interest. And it is that area that we should explore with the patience and assiduity of a paleontologist on an important dig. For it is a region of great potential. Somewhere within it we can find an avenue of interest that so perfectly matches our natural abilities that we will be able to make our greatest contribution and spend our lives in work we thoroughly enjoy.

Sir William Osier, the great physician, was a River Person. He was speaking to other possible River People when he said:

> Throw away, in the first place, all ambition beyond that of doing the day's work well. Find your way into work in which there is an enjoyment of it and all shadows of annoyance seem to flee away. Let each day's work absorb your energy and satisfy your wildest ambition. Success in the long run depends on endurance and perseverance. All

things come to him who has learned to labor and wait, whose talents develop in the still and quiet years of unselfish work.

If you find yourself saying, "I must not be a River Person," wait. Think about it. Examine your life, your wants, your dreams, your daydreams, your visions. And look for a consistent key, a way in which you like to see yourself doing some particular thing as a form of work or service. A consistent daydream is often our inner intelligence trying to tell us what we should be doing. It may be that you are already in the general area you want to be in but just haven't seen its true possibilities. Discontented actors have found their Rivers in directing; discontented salespeople in sales management, and so on. Every industry has within it hundreds, if not thousands, of possibilities. There is advertising and art, public relations, purchasing—the list goes on and on. But keep this in mind: If it's the right work for you, chances are you've found yourself fooling around with it in your spare time in some way, or reading about it, or doodling about it, or visiting it in your free time. Look for a consistent interest. If you find it, you may have found your River. A River in carpentry is just as richly satisfying and fraught with possibilities as any other calling.

If we cannot find a special interest in a particular line of work, then we no doubt should become Goal People. There are those of us who seem to be able to do many things with equal facility and equal interest and enjoyment. There are, for example, professional business executives who simply love the challenge of business. They can take an ailing company and within a few years raise it to a level among the leaders. The company's product or service doesn't seem to make very much difference.

Lee Iacocca was known as an automobile man because of his many successful years at the Ford Motor Company. As such, he was asked to take over the Chrysler Corporation when it was in danger of complete collapse. That he did in a masterful, skillful way. That he risked his professional reputation in the process was an indication of his confidence. The rest of the story is history. But Lee Iacocca might have done just as well taking over a corporation that manufactured toys, copiers, computers, or whatever. Iacocca is a consummate American business executive—he revels in a challenge and in the resulting success and all that goes with it—the big money, the publicity, even the opportunity to run for president of the United States. Iacocca is a Goal Person.

Many will ask, "Why set goals at all? Why not just take things as they come and do your best with what you have 'been given' to do?" That "been given" business is often a way of saying you stumbled into a chance opportunity for work and simply stayed there.

A goal gives a picture to the human subconscious. Everyone has goals, whether he or she will admit it or not. Whatever you want to bring about in your life is a goal: that dress, that sports car, that condominium apartment in Florida, that home in Martha's Vineyard, that man or woman you want to date. Wants are goals. But it seems that for most people, wants seldom get focused on sufficiently or get mixed with enough positive expectation. "I want a lot of things," someone will say.

Without a goal we are much like the man with a boat and nowhere to go. Goals give us the drive and energy we need to remain on the track long enough for their accomplishment. Like the captain of the ship about to leave port, we should be able to tell anyone our next port of call—and perhaps the one after that too. If you have done much traveling at sea, perhaps you were surprised at first by how slowly the ship moved through the water. In a time when it's common for us to drive at sixty and seventy miles per hour and eat lunch while tearing through the sky at six hundred miles per hour, a ship pulling away from a dock and heading for a distant port at twenty knots may seem painfully slow indeed. But the ship moves steadily, twenty-four hours a day, always on course, and the cumulative effect of such relentless singleness of purpose delivers us to the next port of call in a surprisingly short time. One day we raise the distant shore, and soon we're in the harbor, mission accomplished. Now, after refueling perhaps, and the scheduled stop, a new port of call must be determined.

People with goals on which they have set their hearts and minds are always moving toward those goals. Even while we sleep, our deep minds are working on the project. That's why we often awaken, early in the morning, with the solution to a problem that had repeatedly resisted our conscious attempts to solve it the day before. We think about our goal as we have our morning coffee and breakfast, while we're in the shower, and it comes to us again and again during the day. We are on course. We are moving toward the fulfillment of our current goal. And it is often the last thing we think about as we drop off to sleep. It is our aiming point. And people with aiming points tend to reach them.

It's interesting—and often quite astonishing—that people with goals tend to live longer than people without them. It's as if they can extend their lives simply because they have something to do. It must be the interest that lends vitality and energy to their lives.

There are fine old ships, beautifully maintained, still safely sailing the world's seas. They have successfully visited thousands of ports of call. There have been storms at sea and occasional breakdowns of one kind or another, delays when they have had to anchor offshore for a while. But the life of each of these ships has been one of one success after another. That's the way goal-oriented people spend their lives. Each goal, successfully reached, finds them better equipped, with more experience, to set the next goal. Goals for such people tend to ascend in stair-like fashion, each one a bit more demanding and fulfilling than the one before. In a few years they find themselves accomplishing, with surprising ease, goals that would have been impossible for them when they first began their journey into meaning.

Cervantes wrote: "The journey is better than the inn." It's good to rest at the inn after a long journey, just as it's good for our ship to tie up at a dock for a few days' rest after a long sea voyage. But Cervantes was certainly right—the journey is better than the inn. The journey is life and experience; it puts us in the way of new interests and the most astonishing synchronicity. When a person knows where he or she is going and is engaged in getting there, the most amazing coincidences begin to take place. It's like reading something by Victor Hugo—the coincidences often take on the most outrageous appropriateness. Just as we're stumped, that one person with the answers happens along, or someone sends us the one book that has exactly the answer we were looking for. When we know where we're going and are occupied on our journey, it seems as if all the forces, whatever they are, come to our aid. We are helped along by invisible as well as visible sources. This is not to say that we encounter only smooth sailing; on the contrary, there will be a door like that of an exclusive club with a Members Only sign on it. It seems to exist to prevent all but the hundred percenters from gaining entrance. Perseverance—dogged, unflagging, repeatedly rejected perseverance—is the answer, of course, and when we've set our heart and mind on something that is so important to us, we can generate that kind of persistence.

Quite often, if we read a story with the kind of coincidences that are often a part of a goal-oriented person's life, we would put it down, muttering, "Impossible!" But astonishing as it may seem—and astonishing as it sometimes seems to those of us in pursuit of a goal—that kind of synchronicity becomes an active part of the goal-oriented person's life. I say *synchronicity* rather than *coincidence* because I believe it is more than coincidence. It is a meshing, a coalescing of the parts necessary to the successful achievement of our goal. Sometimes it is baffling indeed and often leads us in a circuitous journey. A minor accident, or what appears to be a significant setback, turns out to be necessary if we're to get back on the right track.

But as Emerson wrote, "Trust thyself! Every heart vibrates to that iron string." We should learn to stay on the alert for serendipitous occurrences, accept them, and realize they are a part of the journey toward a goal—another reason why the road is better than the inn. We should not attempt to force such things; we must learn, as the Taoist reminds us, not to push the River. Stay on course, but go with the flow; the right things will happen at the right time, without forcing, without impatience. And we will find ourselves with our goal realized one fine day, just as we'll raise the coastline of the port toward which our ship is churning, or our sailboat sailing. There it is! And we shield our eyes from the early sun and stand at the rail and imagine we can smell the land and hear the sounds of the busy harbor. Soon we're tied up at the pier, our latest journey a success. Now it's time to relax, enjoy the achievement, and rest for a while.

I'm a golf fan, and I've always enjoyed watching the way the great players address and hit the ball. I haven't noticed him doing it lately, but in the days when he was breaking all the records, Jack Nicklaus had a most interesting style. He would take his stance at the ball and look at the spot on the fairway or the green where he wanted his ball to land. Then he would look at a point some six to ten feet in front of his ball, then at the ball—then at the point six to ten feet away, then at the point again on the fairway or green. He always seemed to have an intermediate point over which he wanted the ball to pass: he always had two aiming points—one quite close, the other where he wanted his ball to land. When he was ready—and not a moment before—he would uncork that legendary swing of his that left the gallery gasping and whooping with admiration and amazement.

Intermediate aiming points are often important to identify and establish on the way to any sort of really substantial goal. We know what our ultimate

landing site is. We have established that—*but where do we begin?* That's where intermediate goals come into the picture. Quite often it is these intermediate goals on which people are reluctant to spend enough time. These are often the core skills vital to the completion of the final project. Here we find the person who wants to amaze friends with his or her skill at the piano but doesn't want to put in the time and effort required to learn to play well. This is the person who is forever looking for shortcuts. This person is a great daydreamer—but when it comes down to the nitty-gritty of the intermediate goals—ah, that's too difficult or boring or time-consuming. There are millions of fat people looking for a twelve-day miracle that will magically restore them to their perfect weight. But suggest they follow a regimen or learn new habits that will take off a pound a week for a year and at the same time cause them to put together a new lifestyle that will keep them trim for the rest of their lives—it's no deal. They don't want to change their eating habits;

they only want to change their weight and appearance. So they remain fat.

Want to be a writer? How about spending some time studying the English language? How about reading some really good books? Spend a couple of years putting some real quality into your education!

Want to get rich in real estate? Learn the business first. The first step of the successful Goal Person is *commitment.* The person who is 100 percent committed to the achievement of a goal is quite willing to take whatever intermediate steps are necessary. The bridges are burned; there is no escape route on which to come tiptoeing back when things get rough. Commitment, 100 percent.

When that happens, the goal is as good as accomplished, and you'll have fun and great experiences on the road to its achievement. In fact, the goal itself may come as an anticlimax, demanding the immediate setting of a new goal. People who know such committed persons and are privy to their goals also know they will reach those goals. They become silent and affirmative partners and often set in motion events that will help along the way.

As we work to bring a difficult long-range goal to reality, we gradually grow into the kind of people for whom such goals are natural. That's because before we can *do* something, we must *be* something. And to me, this way we have of growing to fit the work, the social situation involved, the embodiment of superior achievement, are mind-boggling wonders. We actually become what we think about. And the key to it all is that each of us must do the thinking; each of us has his or her own governor tied to his or her own innate capabilities. I could no more do the things Lee Iacocca does than the pelicans that fly past my balcony every afternoon could fly backward. I don't set the same goals Iacocca sets.

I cannot set your goals any more than you can set mine. You are the only person alive who can set your goals, although others may inspire you from time to time to do more than you might have done without their encouragement. Encouragement is the function of a good leader, a coach, or manager. The presence of an inspired and dedicated leader can significantly upgrade the performance of a large corporation employing thousands of men and women. Hence the saying that the success or failure of any organization is but the lengthened shadow of its leader.

But the point I want to make here is that we all have basic and inherent genetic differences. I knew a corporal in the Marine Corps during World War II who could perform the most astonishing tricks with his mind. Whenever some kind of test was ordered, he easily outscored everyone else on the base, if not in the entire corps. Both his mother and father were full professors at leading universities. He came from a long line of people with high IQs and as a result could think rings around most of the rest of us and do mathematical problems in his head that we couldn't have done under any circumstances. He had inherited a sixteen-cylinder brain. Our species needs such people for the special tasks they perform. There are also a lot of eight and six and four-cylinder brains, and we need those too. And the most fascinating point of all this is that regardless of the genetic equipment we've been handed, the goals we set—and invariably reach when they are truly our goals and not the goals of a parent or acquaintance—meet our desires perfectly. We are quite happy with them.

The house and neighborhood that represent complete success and total satisfaction to one person might represent failure to another; they also might be the kind of home and grounds that most people are quite content simply to drive past with exclamations of wonder and delight.

That's why I have stressed that you examine your daydreams for signs of a repetitive picture. It may be the aiming point for the present. Just as coughing is the only way the lungs can beg a smoker to stop destroying them, our daydreams or habitual visions are often the way our inherent genetic mix is put together;

those dreams and visions are trying to tell us which way to go. They are often the projection of our inner voice. And that inner voice is based on very sound judgment about our true inherent capacities.

One thing we must put aside in order to fulfill our unique possibilities is conformity. We all conform in hundreds of ways. Even those of us who feel we have gone our own individual ways in the world, who have lived more or less as free and independent spirits, are conformists to an extent that would surprise us if those ways were listed and printed out for us. But we need to recognize that there are ways in which we must not conform. And we need to recognize the fact that the tendency to conform to the standards of others without question is insidious and ever-present. There is a human tendency, no doubt acquired and strengthened in childhood, to believe that whatever people in significant numbers are doing must be correct or so many of them wouldn't be doing it. That statement may never be spoken or thought in just that way, but I'm sure you

know what I mean. When I was a youngster, popular things were believed to be best. Florsheim shoes were thought to be the best, as were Hart, Shaffner, and Marx suits—not that I ever owned either during that time. My father and no doubt hundreds of thousands in similar situations felt that Pontiac was the best car—but earlier it had been Buick, and before that, a Reo Flying Cloud. There were popular fads, and unless one conformed to them, one simply wasn't "in," or later, "hip." To flash the proper label indicated that you were knowledgeable about what to wear and drive.

The fact is, they were all wrong. The popular, heavily advertised brands were fine and suited the great masses of people quite handily, but they really were not the best that money could buy. The great majority of people seldom enjoy the best of anything. They don't drink the best scotch or bourbon, wear the best clothes or shoes, or drive the best cars. The best is never the most popular.

I mention these things to establish the importance

of questioning the things we do. Do we do them because they are what "everybody else is doing" or because we have come to the conclusion that they are best for us and our personal journey into meaning?

To young people, the need to belong is paramount. The group is the thing, and to be a member of the group is quite sufficient—so sufficient that one is willing to lose every vestige of individuality and take on the trappings, speech, and habits of the group. "Oh, God, just let me belong!" is the unspoken prayer. And that's fine. It's their first true identity outside their families, and it's important. That it takes them far afield of what their parents traditionally expected is better yet. Outraging or at least amazing their parents is an important part of the act. And of course it is an act. Just as the thousands of college students on spring break who inundate the Fort Lauderdale, Florida waterfront are expressing their break with the polite routine of the family and their younger days. They are expressing their freedom from the family and from all other rules of human conduct by joining another group. They are still as individually faceless as they were before, perhaps more so, they are like a herd of white-faced Herefords, virtually indistinguishable from one another. But this passage rite is important to them. Fine. But after it, each of them must find his or her own pathway in the world; however, it is my observation that very few of them do. They simply leave one group to join another, and although they will soon put aside childish and primitive activities (destroying and vandalizing the property of others is typical), chances are they will still represent a group and will act in unison in most ways. They will tend to live in tract homes or condominium apartments with all the charm and creative touches of an army barracks, and they will spend their entire lives taking their cues from their peer group. Reisman called it *other-directed*, as opposed to *inner-directed* behavior. Until we begin living as inner-directed persons, we follow others who are, in turn, following us. Maybe there isn't a leader up there somewhere at all but rather just a huge circle with everybody following everybody else.

Although there are possibly exceptions—I have never found one—a good rule to follow is:

> **Whatever the majority of people is doing, under any given circumstance, if you do the exact opposite, you will probably never make another mistake as long as you live.**

You can apply it to education, driving your car, obtaining a job, or waiting until you find the woman or man who will be your companion for the rest of your life.

You and I are going to make a lot of mistakes along the way. One of the worst mistakes will be to get in our own way, that is, to override our real intelligence with expediency and the desire to conform with the rest of the people. If you do it with your golf swing, you get a ruined shot—not too bad, although a frustrating disappointment. If you do it while driving your car, it can kill you or someone else. And if you do it enough with your daily life—forget it.

We need to calm down, relax more, and smile more. Pick that spot on the fairway or on the green where you want that lovely little ball to land, and then when you're ready, hit the ball.

River Person or Goal Person—and sometimes a combination of both—is the way to go. In the words of Robert Schuller, "God's word for today: find the gift that is in you."

2.

STAY WITH IT

I always felt I was pretty good in the perseverance department. After all, writing a radio program every day for twenty-six years—that's about nine thousand radio programs, researched or thought of and then written one word at a time on a typewriter before being recorded for broadcast—6,300,000 words, one word at a time. It doesn't exactly label me a fly-by-night kind of person. But when it comes to perseverance, compared to my wife Diana, I'm still in kindergarten.

She is simply implacable. So between us, setting and reaching goals, no matter what their degree of difficulty, is not a matter for questioning. *We do it.*

We've all seen motion pictures in which the hero, mustering that last cubic centimeter of strength, crawls over the final sand dune to see—to his delighted astonishment—a shady oasis with abundant fresh water and the cheerful leader of a camel train who volunteers to give him a free ride back to civilization and ultimate victory. It is mustering that last bit of energy, for just one more try and then, after that, just one more, that often leads to victory in real life.

"Nothing takes the place of persistence." Do you remember that little essay President Calvin Coolidge made so popular? It's true—nothing takes the place of persistence, once you know that what you're seeking is right for you.

When I resigned my cushy job at CBS in Chicago in 1950 and started my own program on WGN, I also agreed to help sell time on my show by calling on advertising agencies. So I would write my next day's program at home at night, then first thing the next morning I would start hitting the advertising agencies to tell them why their clients should be advertising on my daily radio program. I was completely unknown in the Chicago market or anywhere else; my time on the air amounted to just fifteen minutes each afternoon. My prospects would say, "No, sorry, your program is not in 'drive time'"—a ridiculous cliché, since at any time in Chicago there were a zillion cars on the roads and highways, to say nothing of the ten zillion people listening to their radios at home in about a six-state area. But that's the kind of answer I got, so I became acquainted with the word *no*. After making calls on numerous agencies and getting nothing but nos, I would then rush to my tiny office in the Tribune Tower, get my program ready for broadcasting, and when the red light came on, I had to be cheerful!

Month after month I made the rounds, and as I did, my thoughts often drifted back to those untroubled days in the quiet, air-conditioned studios at CBS, when all that was expected of me was the occasional exercise of my larynx.

Stay with it, I would tell myself. One time I surprised a gentleman standing next to me in the men's room of a Chicago high-rise by actually muttering it aloud.

"What was that? Sorry, I didn't hear you very well," he said.

"What? Oh! Nothing. Nothing at all. Just talking to myself, I suppose," I responded.

Embarrassing, yes, but no less important for that. *Stay with it!* I knew that if I could just stay with it long enough to earn the respect and notice of the Chicago advertising community, I could succeed at my project. *Stay with it*, I would say to myself on those cold, snowy mornings and hot, humid summer days. *Stay with it*, I would say to myself on those heartbreakingly beautiful mornings when all in the world I wanted to do was play hooky, play golf, or walk along the lakefront in the park. So I made my calls and I broadcast my programs and

I heard otherwise intelligent agency people say to me, "Radio doesn't work for us."

I would then say, "When you say 'Radio doesn't work for us,' it's the same as a commanding general saying, 'Tanks don't work for us,' or 'Air strikes don't work for us.' The effective commander makes best use of all forces available to him, and so does the good advertising executive. What do you mean, 'Radio doesn't work for us'? What radio? Which radio? Which program or personality? Surely some facet of an industry as broad, pervasive, and successful as American radio will work for you. In fact, my program will work for you in Chicago; I will see to it that my program does a good job for you and returns sales in many times the volume of its small cost."

So I would win the argument and lose the sale. Once he had made his statement, he had to stand behind it or run the risk of being a reasonable, flexible, intelligent advertising executive, and that was, indeed, a great deal to expect.

It was in Kroch's Book Store on Michigan Avenue that I found the copy of *Think and Grow Rich* by Napoleon Hill, in which I found the six-word secret to success I had been searching for for so many years. I took the book back into Kroch's bookstore and pigeon-holed Adolph Kroch himself.

"Buy time on my radio program, and I'll sell this book by the thousands of copies," I said.

"We've tried radio. It doesn't work for us," he replied.

"Don't confuse my radio program with the word 'radio.' My program will work for you with this book and with other books in your store as well."

"I'll tell you what I'll do," he said. "I'll give forty cents a copy for every copy of the book you sell."

I was not supposed to work on commission; I was supposed to bring in contracts: thirteen-week, twenty-six-week, or fifty-two-week contracts.

"You've got a deal," I said.

Not since the publication of *Gone with the Wind*

had old man Kroch seen orders for a book come in the way they came in for the next few weeks. As he wrote out my very sizable checks for thousands of orders at forty cents a copy, he wished he'd followed my advice and simply bought airtime on my program; it would have been infinitely cheaper. He promptly rectified the matter. I got him to write a letter saying what my program had accomplished for him, and from that time on, with the kind of proof that the followers of the world need before they will make a move, my program began to attract sponsors. It grew from fifteen minutes a day to a half-hour, then to a full hour, then to an hour in the afternoon and a half-hour in the morning, then to an additional half-hour daily television program—all happily sponsored.

On the program I talked about things I found to be interesting: books, philosophy, people, and events. My only rule for subject matter was that it had to be interesting to me. If it was interesting to me, I felt it would be interesting to a large section of the radio audience, and I was right. I have long thought it shameful the way the broadcasting industry has underestimated the listener. I think the radio listener wants more than repeated news, weather, and music. Radio is certainly one of the greatest educational opportunities in the world, the only rule being: *Keep it interesting.*

My habit of muttering to myself *Stay with it!* had paid off, just as it always does. The world is full of those who "tried" to get out of the doldrums and, meeting with difficulty and repeated turndowns, retreated back to the big crowd. What's really amazing are the number who have made sorties into a business of their own, then failed and fell back, never to try again. Why should succeeding at a business of one's own be easier than learning to ski or play the piano? We are likely to fail at first—it's part of the learning process—but it's no reason to give up. We learn something important from every failure; it's staying with it that separates the winners from the losers.

And *staying with it* applies to so much that is

good and healthful in life. Failures aren't the end of the world—they are far from it. If they were, no human being would ever learn to walk or speak or ride a bicycle or obtain an education. We take early failures for granted in so many things, yet when we attempt something as adults, we become self-conscious. We become concerned about what our friends and acquaintances might think.

Perseverance is another word for *faith*!

Many years ago I was riding in a taxi in Chicago's Loop. I remember the spot well: Marshall Field's department store was there on the right. My driver commented that a friend of his, another cab driver, had started to go into a business of his own.

"But I talked him out of it," my driver said. "I told him that 95 percent of all new businesses fail and that he'd lose his shirt."

"What did he do?" I asked.

"He's back to drivin' a cab where he belongs." My driver chuckled.

"Where did you get the statistic that 95 percent of all new business ventures fail?" I asked.

"What? Why, everybody knows that," he countered.

"You were wrong. Ninety-five percent of new businesses do not fail. And let me ask you this: If your friend had gone into a business of his own and failed, could he have got his job back driving a cab?" I asked.

"Oh, sure," he answered.

"Then he didn't have anything to lose by trying, did he?" I asked.

"He might have lost some money," he observed.

"But what if he had succeeded? What if he had found his way out of cab driving into a successful and prosperous career as a businessman, like Marshall Field or the founders of all the businesses in Chicago? You didn't do him a favor, you kept him from what might have been a wonderful success," I said.

The silence, even in Chicago's Loop, was suddenly deafening.

"I guess I didn't think of it like that."

"Giving advice to friends doesn't require thinking," I commented. "All you have to do is open your mouth, and all the clichés and myths and half-truths just come pouring out. I heard it all as a kid."

"You have your own business?"

"Yes, I do."

He just shook his head.

Friends often seem to have a vested interest in keeping us in their company. Any talk on our part of doing something that will elevate us to a new plateau can start the myth machine. That is not true with special friends. There are friends who are completely unselfish in their desire to see us do well, who take pride in our accomplishments. But when you get advice, consider the source. What are his or her qualifications for commenting on something you want very much to do? Best of all, don't talk about it! Just do it. And if it fails, do it again and again until you get it right. If you've made up your mind to do something, and if you are fully committed, you're going to do it. A year or so devoted to planning, studying, and marshaling your resources is certainly a good idea.

The story of success in all fields is the story of persistence, perseverance, doggedness, bullheadedness, stubbornness, and tenaciousness. *There!* That should handle the matter.

But as Eric Hoffer wrote:

> There are many who find a good alibi far more attractive than an achievement. For an achievement does not settle anything permanently. We still have to prove that we are as good today as we were yesterday.
>
> But when we have a valid alibi for not achieving anything, we are fixed, so to speak, for life. Moreover, when we have an alibi for not writing a book and not painting a picture and so on, we have an alibi for not writing the greatest book and not painting the greatest picture. Small wonder that the effort expended and the punishment

> **endured in obtaining a good alibi often exceed the effort and grief requisite for the attainment of a most marked achievement.**

How true that is! We've all seen men begging for money with physical handicaps no worse than those suffered by many who are working hard and supporting a family. For one, it's a reason to try all the harder; for the other, it's an alibi for begging.

I'm sure we're all guilty from time to time of using convenient alibis for not doing some of the things we might do. But if we're honest with ourselves, we don't make it a way of life. But there are many who do just that and live lives far below the levels of attainment they might know. They cling to their alibis frantically, with both hands, forcing themselves to close their eyes and ears to the truth that surges about them.

One time the late Dr. Maxwell Maltz, the plastic surgeon who achieved a great deal of fame through his book *Psycho-Cybernetics*, dropped by my office for a chat and lunch. We fell to talking about his favorite subject—namely, how a person can come to grips with himself or herself, develop a healthy self-image, and find freedom in the world.

At that time, Dr. Maltz, whom we called Uncle Max, was seventy-two years old. He was as busy as he had ever been in his life, traveling from one end of the world to the other, making speeches, returning to his New York offices for surgery commitments, and starting all sorts of new projects along the way.

He told me he had discovered four important steps that a person can take on a regular basis to form new habits that can build a healthy new self-image. As he talked at lunch, I made notes. Here are his four points in the order in which he gave them to me:

1 FORGIVE OTHERS, WITH NO STRINGS ATTACHED. Clean the slate absolutely by forgiving every person against whom you might hold some kind of grudge. Do this for your own sake, your own peace of mind. We don't hurt others when we hold hatred toward them; we hurt ourselves. And we can hurt ourselves seriously by allowing hatred to fester in our consciousness. So forgive others—all others. If you cannot take this first step, you can forget the rest—you haven't grown up yet.

2 FORGIVE YOURSELF. See yourself with kind eyes. Try to forget completely all the idiotic things you've done, the pain you've given to others, the embarrassments you've suffered, the mistakes you've made in the past. Again, wipe the slate clean. Look in the mirror and forgive yourself. Practice this, and you can actually pull it off. It's not easy to forgive ourselves. We are our own worst critics, and we can be much tougher on ourselves than we are on others. But the fact is, blame doesn't help—it's a destructive emotion.

3 **SEE YOURSELF AT YOUR BEST.** As Dr. Maltz put it, "We can start the day in frustration or confidence, take your pick. The intelligent thing to do is pick confidence, if it's at all possible." There are bad days, but it's better to begin the day in a confident mood than in a mood of frustration.

4 **KEEP UP WITH YOURSELF.** Don't worry about what others are doing or what others have. Keep your pace—it's different from the pace of others. It's faster than some, slower than others. Forget the Joneses, and don't feel guilty about moving ahead of some of your contemporaries. The person who deliberately holds himself down to a slower pace just to be one of the gang is a fool. Keep up with yourself. Live the life you want to live; earn what you want to earn; do what you want to do. Live your own life, and don't be too concerned about how others are living theirs.

Max told me that day at lunch that he called these the four steps to a healthy self-image:

 Forgive others.

 Forgive yourself.

3 See yourself at your best—choose confidence instead of frustration.

4 Keep up with yourself, march to your own drummer, go at your own pace, and don't worry about what others are doing.

Very good advice from a distinguished physician.

You may wonder why a cosmetic surgeon, a man who put people back together after accidents and gun battles, was so interested in the idea of self-esteem. It was because he found in his practice that although he could remove disfiguring scars, birthmarks, and other anomalies from the faces and bodies of his patients, they often kept the same crippled opinions of themselves even after the surgery had healed. And when that happened, the surgery had failed. He found that unless he could change the inner person to match the new outer person, the individual remained crippled. It's another area where perseverance is required. And as we grow into new persons, achieving ever-higher goals, we need to become on the inside the person we are becoming on the outside.

Staying with our plans despite repeated setbacks tends to build inner character, just as it draws maturity on our faces.

I came across a story about a boy named Sparky. School was all but impossible for Sparky. He failed every subject in the eighth grade. He flunked physics in high school. Receiving a flat zero in the course, he distinguished himself as the worst physics student in the school's history. He also flunked Latin and algebra and English. He didn't do much better in sports.

Although he did manage to make the school golf team, he promptly lost the only important match of the year. There was a consolation match. He lost that too.

Throughout his youth, Sparky was awkward socially. He was not actually disliked by the other students; no one cared that much. He was astonished if a classmate ever said hello to him outside school hours. No way to tell how he might have done at dating. In high school, Sparky never once asked a girl out. He was too afraid of being turned down.

Sparky was a loser. He, his classmates—everyone knew it. So he rolled with it. Sparky made up his mind early in life that if things were meant to work out, they would. Otherwise he would content himself with what appeared to be his inevitable mediocrity.

But one thing was important to Sparky: drawing. He was proud of his own artwork. Of course, no one else appreciated it. In his senior year of high school, he submitted some cartoons to the editors of his class yearbook. They were turned down. Despite this particularly painful rejection, Sparky was so convinced of his ability that he decided to become a professional artist.

Upon graduating from high school, he wrote a letter to Walt Disney Studios. He was told to send some samples of his artwork, and the subject matter for a cartoon was suggested. Sparky drew the proposed cartoon. He spent a great deal of time on it and on the other drawings. Finally the reply from Walt Disney Studios came—he had been rejected once again. Another loss for the loser.

So Sparky wrote his own autobiography in cartoons. He described his childhood self, a little-boy loser and chronic under-achiever. The cartoon character would soon become famous all over the world. For Sparky, the boy who failed every subject in the eighth grade and whose work was rejected again and again was Charles Schulz. He created the *Peanuts* comic strip and the little cartoon boy whose kite would never fly and who never succeeded in kicking the football—Charlie Brown.

Perseverance—nothing can take its place. There is a place for every person who will persevere; there is a large success lurking in everything we do. And it's not just our success we're talking about here. Millions of people have been cheered by and seen themselves in Charlie Brown. There's a Lucy who will snatch that football away in every neighborhood. She's a good girl, really; she just loves to frustrate Charlie Brown. Charles Schulz succeeded beyond his most sanguine imagination, and he earned and deserved that success. Perhaps he failed at everything else he tried because his talent and humor were so complete, so wonderfully successful, when he finally found what it was he was supposed to do.

We tend to be an instant gratification society. Pick the home of your choice and pay for it later—the same with the car, the furniture, the clothes, and the jewelry. Instant coffee and frozen foods—all wonderfully efficient boons to modern living. But some things don't change. It takes time to become very good at something. Young stars in major sports who are paid those astronomical salaries and bonuses have been playing those sports, and playing them exceedingly well, for many years.

"Not for me," you and I say, and I think we're right. I want to spend time on the golf course and on my boat. I want to do some traveling, and I like to have the time to buy things, not just earn money. But when I work, I work hard, and I stay with and finish what I begin. Most of all, I want to spend time with Diana. I enjoy her company. I can't do all those things and work eighteen hours a day. I can do all I need to do in a good solid six hours a day, sitting at my typewriter and poking about in my research library. That often includes Saturday and Sunday, but it still leaves plenty of time for other interests.

There seems to be a door on the way to remarkable success that can be passed through only by those willing to persevere beyond the point where the majority stop and turn back. Few of us realize in the early days how long it takes to succeed in an extraordinary way. And it should take sufficient time. It is a process of preparation, testing, and retesting, a process of growth and education, so that when we do pass through that door into the interesting and gratifying realm beyond, we are qualified and bear the scars of repeated attempts. We are initiated, quite thoroughly.

But time will pass anyway, whether we do or do not, so it makes sense to stay with it, to hang on for a while longer and get in the habit of surmounting challenges; there will be more of them up the road. Problems don't end with our first success. Problems are integral to living. Successful people are not people without problems—they are people who have learned to solve their problems.

People say, "I need to make some money!" The only people who make money are people who work in the mint. They take very special paper, very special inks, and very special engraving, and they manufacture—actually make—money. That's how they earn their living. And like them, we must earn ours. And just as it would be better if, instead of saying, "I need a job," we said, "I must find a way of being of service," it would be a good idea to say, "I need to earn some money." It changes the entire attitude. Many do say it that way, and they succeed in earning the money they need.

Early in this chapter I talked about starting my own radio program on WGN Chicago and how difficult it was to sell time on the program in the beginning. Let me point out that in 1950, television was still rather new. It was so exciting and important a medium that for a long time it seriously overshadowed radio in the minds of the advertising community. Much the same thing happened when radio was invented. Everyone was saying, "Who'd buy a newspaper when you can get the news instantaneously and free just by owning a radio?" But newspapers still flourish, of course, and offer a great deal that isn't found on radio or television. Similarly, radio, the most ubiquitous and pervasive medium of them all, is alive and well. Radio stations

have flourished and multiplied, and even if they were only listened to by the drivers of automobiles, they would still be a good advertising buy. But radio is much more than that. The quality of an advertisement determines its effect, and the same is true for radio stations.

Television is not "better than" radio by any means. I recall the years when I was the voice of *Sky King* on radio. It was a highly rated network kid's show, and we regularly performed feats of derring-do on the radio program that would have been impossible in those days on television. I recall one episode in which I was fighting an arch-criminal on the wing of a jet airplane. We wore suction cups on our shoes, if my memory serves, and thanks to our talented sound effects man, it sounded to millions of kids as if we were doing just that. As the jet sped through the air at high speed and at a considerable altitude, with sounds of the air roaring, the jet engine screaming, the loud suction cups plopping about, and the two combatants grunting, I was successful in vanquishing my wily foe. But not until

Mike Wallace had interrupted to sell Peter Pan Peanut Butter. And sell it he did. At that time practically all television was live, and we found ourselves saying after the program, "Let them try that on television!"

And today, as I write these words, my syndicated daily radio commentary is heard on hundreds of radio stations throughout the United States, Canada, Mexico City, Australia, New Zealand, South Africa, the beautiful Bahamas, and many places in between. None of which would have happened if, years ago, I hadn't kept muttering to myself, *Stay with it!* Just the other day, I received a letter from our station in Guam inviting Diana and me to share Thanksgiving Day with them. Radio is not only alive and well—it is simply everywhere! My induction into the Radio Hall of Fame in the spring of 1986 was one of the real highlights of my life.

Spending time with Diana

THE ADVENTURES OF SKY KING

Earl, as Sky King (far right)
Clipper, Penny, and ranch foreman, Jill Bell.

3.

FINDING A BALANCE

Who succeeds in America, and why?

The person who succeeds in America is the person who sets his or her own wages, goals, and lifestyle. Successful people are those who discover that life is ready and willing to meet their requirements. They set their incomes to meet their needs and wants by discovering within themselves a marketable factor and developing that factor to whatever degree necessary in order to derive the appropriate reward response.

Unsuccessful people are those who make their life-styles fit whatever wages they receive. They put themselves on the receiving end of things and have little to say about their own economic welfare.

Successful people put themselves behind the wheel of their lives; the unsuccessful ride in the passenger seats.

Almost everything has an economic base today. We are rewarded by the amount of money we receive for what we do. What we do in a free society, and what we charge for what we do in a free society, are largely matters of personal choice.

If we discover our best opportunities for personal expression are within the framework of a large corporation, we can so develop and apply ourselves as to reach whatever levels of accomplishment and reward we are willing to reach.

It takes time to succeed—and it should. We need to earn our stripes through the daily passage of time and experience so that each successive step is accepted and applauded by those who have come to know us. Meaningful and richly rewarding journeys take time. They take preparation and careful planning, and—as every seasoned traveler knows—they are subject to the vagaries of incident and the mistakes and inefficiencies of others along the way. But although the journey has its adventures and misadventures, it also has a definite upward momentum, and there is no doubting its eventual destination—the goal of the person in command. Each new upward step along the way prepares our resolute traveler for the next plateau. And if he or she does not lose the exciting vision of the goal to be reached or meet with an untimely end (the silent tragedy of war and accident), the goal, with all the trimmings and more, will be his or hers.

Remember Cervantes's words, "The journey is better than the inn." The journey is our life, our holiday on earth, our time here, as we successively set new goals or dive back into our great rivers of interest—or both!

We receive what we fully expect to receive—and usually a good deal more. We become what we think about.

We become successful to the extent of our true desires and determination. And we do so by building on our strong point, our *forte*.

What is your forte? You should know what it is by now. At what are you best? What gives you the most, the deepest satisfaction? Whatever that is can be honed to marketable proportions in some way and applied in service to others to earn you the rewards you seek and should have and will have.

And that's your part of the bargain. No one is supposed to do that for you, or hold your hand, or rush to your aid every time you slip or fall back a little. That's the earning part that falls on each of us. There is help enough on every side if we are wise enough and energetic enough to make use of it—help in the form of books or recorded cassette programs such as those produced by my company. And there are the numerous people who come to our aid once we're on course. But such people need not be sought or importuned. They come of their own natural need, like magic, at just the right time. Events begin to fall into our lives like missing pieces of a jigsaw puzzle. Such good fortune is the mark of a person with the attitude that tells the world that he or she knows where he or she is going and fully expects to get there. They approach their commitments "with intentionality and delight," as my friend Dr. Charles Garfield puts it in his book and audio program, *Peak Performance*.

The distinguished Dr. Abraham Maslow put it this way: "If you deliberately plan to be less than you are capable of being, then I warn you that you will be unhappy for the rest of your life. You'll be evading your own capacities, your own possibilities."

And let me add this: If you think you can succeed in a large way and play it safe at the same time, you are sadly mistaken. Success takes risk; it takes full commitment. You go out on a limb, so to speak, and take your chances alone. The warm, comfortable, huddling masses must be left behind along with the old neighborhood and the small dreams. Risk and success are at opposite ends of the same balancing beam. You cannot have one without the corresponding weight of the other. Risk ups the ante, raises the greens fee, and limits the membership. But it makes playing more fun, and you seldom have to wait in line anymore.

The late motion picture producer Mike Todd put it well. He said, "Being broke is a temporary situation; being poor is a state of mind."

Who has success in America? Or in Canada, Mexico, or Peru, or in France or West Germany or Japan? Or anywhere else? Those who have taken charge of their lives and are directing them to their own best use.

Who does not have success? Those persons who have not taken charge of the direction of their lives but have simply reacted to the environment in which they found themselves. They have become a part of it.

Our environment, at any stage of our lives, is a

mirrorlike reflection of ourselves at that time. It may be a transitional stage or, as is more often the case, a permanent statement of ourselves and the extent of our preparation and contribution.

But what about the millions of women whose financial incomes and lifestyles are to a considerable extent determined by the men they have married? Once again, it's the result of a decision on the woman's part. She need not cast her financial lot in life on the ability or ambition of her husband. She has an excellent mind of her own and is free at all times, married or single, to make her own decisions. She can be of enormous help to the marriage partnership by adding her own intelligence, creativity, and talents to the service side. Hundreds of thousands of wives, perhaps millions, are responsible for much, if not most or even all, of the family's success. Women tend to be more practical than men. They also tend to have a better balance between the right and left hemispheres of the brain: high creativity and sound, practical balance. My life, my world, would be a sadly crippled affair without my wife Diana's contribution in every facet of our lives together.

It often happens at public affairs, where I am to be the speaker that because of my life's work, I receive a disproportionate share of the limelight. When I introduce Diana as my wife, I want to tell everyone in attendance—as if I could—how much more she is to me and to our lives together than the familiar word *wife* implies. As I told her one day recently, she is to my life what the sun is to the earth. To ask what share she deserves in our success since our marriage is to ask the impossible. I couldn't have done it without her. She makes it all worthwhile and so much fun. She brings her solid intelligence to bear on all that we do, and her marvelous sense of humor and quick laughter and response are endlessly charming and endearing.

The old cliché, "Behind every successful man there is a good woman," is as ridiculous as it is patronizing. It's as ridiculous as saying, "Behind every man who has failed to be all that he can be is a woman who has failed." There are often wonderful women who share, without complaint, the failures of their husbands, just as there are silly idiotic women behind many successful men and vice versa.

The fact is that men and women come in all possible permutations of the species, and there are no good guidelines or explanations of why certain men marry certain women or vice versa. But rules for achievement have nothing whatever to do with gender. They apply as well and as disinterestedly to women as they do to men: As we sow, so shall we reap. If you want a true assessment of the extent of your service to your fellow human beings, consider the extent of your rewards. You may be underpaid, it's true, but if you accept underpayment, that is your compromise.

People see a successful person living the good life with all the perquisites of modern success and say, "Look at that! Man, would I love to have what he, or she, has. How lucky can you get!?"

Lucky? Luck is what happens when preparedness meets opportunity. People who say such things don't know about the planning, the study, the preparation, the long hours, the hard work, and the steady, implacable resolve. All they see is the end result, and they call it luck.

Many years ago, when I had my own daily radio and television programs on WGN in Chicago, a friend of mine, the sales manager of a Chicago radio station, told me an interesting story at lunch one day. It was about an incident that had occurred the week before at his country club. He had been playing a round of golf with his regular foursome. The tee of one of the holes was contiguous to a main highway. As the foursome approached the tee, they saw a semitrailer rig grind to a stop alongside the tee and a large driver climb down from the cab and lean on the fence—just a few feet from the tee—to watch them hit their tee shots.

Golfers grow accustomed to other members of the club watching them tee off, especially on the first

tee, where there is often a group of members getting ready to play. But this was different. There was hostility crackling in the air as the truck driver looked at the four middle-aged men playing a round of golf on a weekday.

It turned out to be my friend Bill's honor, so he walked to the tee markers, teed up his ball, then stood behind it, sighting down the fairway and taking a couple of easy practice swings. He was trying desperately to regain his concentration. There was no sound from the intently observing truck driver. Bill took his stance, waggled his three wood—a wise choice, under the circumstances—and then, after sighting once again down the fairway, he shot a quick glance at the truck driver. Whereupon the truck driver said, in a loud, clear voice, "Go on! Hit it, you rich son of a bitch!"

And my friend Bill swung his three wood with all the force and power he could muster. The badly topped ball dribbled off the tee. Bill had lost his cool.

"And the tragedy of it all," Bill said that day at lunch, "was that I'm not rich!"

How many times in the discomfort of his post-flub imagination had Bill seen himself hit the best shot of his life—one of those great high arcers—far and away down the center of the fairway as the astonished truck driver looked on with open-mouthed admiration before slouching back to the cab of his truck?

Bill was a typical businessman golfer and a hard-working sales manager. After the truck driver left, following Bill's failure in the spotlight, Bill's friends insisted that he hit a mulligan. They agreed that the leering truck driver was a factor that might have ruined any one of their shots. Besides, he wasn't a natural hazard and as such could be removed before taking the next shot.

But a very interesting story lurks in that incident. Once the truck driver made his outrageous statement, Bill assumed the role of an impostor. He should have backed off before hitting his shot and walked over to the truck driver. He might have said, "My name is Bill Randall [the name is fictitious]. I am not a rich man—far from it. I'm a hardworking radio-station sales manager trying to enjoy a round of golf with some friends. Now if you'll shut up, I'll do my best to make a decent shot."

Then, after setting the record straight, comfortably back in his true identity, chances are Bill would have hit one of his better drives. But Bill, who is of a generation that often viewed rich men in much the same way as the truck driver had, did not refute the "rich son of a bitch" comment and thus had to fail on the shot. He had to show the "rich son of a bitch" in a bad light. And he did.

Had Bill been a rich man and comfortable in the role, he would have hit a good drive, ignoring the truck driver and his rude comment as he might ignore a waiter clearing away the dishes after a business luncheon.

We tend to perform well in the role in which we habitually see ourselves. That's another reason goals are so important. When we seriously establish a difficult goal, we immediately begin to become the person to whom such an achievement would naturally accrue. Bill did not see himself—and had never seen himself—as a rich man. He saw himself in the role he lived, as a sales manager for a big-city radio station, working toward retirement. Bill was successful and content in his role.

He may have idly wished from time to time that he were a rich man, just as the woman wished she could play the piano as beautifully as the visiting concert pianist. But wishes aren't serious goals to which people fully commit themselves. Separating wishes from serious goals is the mark of maturity, and we must be willing to pay the price.

Is it worth it?

Is success, as we've defined it here, worth the trouble, the effort, the commitment, the dedication, the perseverance? Yes. Yes, of course it is worth it. The time will pass anyway, why not put it to constructive, productive use? Everyone benefits, nobody loses.

In the field of human endeavor, it's the successful men and women who make the important difference. They see growth and improvement as the natural order of things, and they can see themselves growing into new arenas of achievement and commensurate reward.

"Only that day dawns to which we are awake," wrote Henry David Thoreau.

What a pity it is for a human being with the gift of consciousness to take life and all that is connected with life for granted—to live each day as his or her due and quite likely find more to criticize than to be grateful for. Yet that is exactly how millions live out their lives. They often give the impression that they have a contract with forever when it is really for only a handful of years. Why not give it all we have to give? Why not make a thorough exploration of ourselves and by so doing find what it is we have to add to the quality somewhere? To make life better because we made an appearance here—to serve in the way we think we can serve best.

Succeeding is so much fun! Especially if it means moving several levels above the one where you spent your youth. For one thing it tells you that you have done a better job of serving the community than your parents. That's progress. Perhaps your children will do a better job of it than you and keep the ball rolling.

Succeeding brings so much of the world within the realm of experience for you. You can actually fly on the Concorde and take a trip on the Orient Express, cruise along the coast of China if you like, or fly over the poles. Succeeding brings the world within range, including much greater success.

Now—let's think in new directions.

How about this idea? Fly to Cannes, France. After a few days on the French Riviera, charter a yacht and spend the next couple of months exploring the coasts of Italy and Yugoslavia and the Greek islands. After making arrangements to charter the boat again next year to continue your explorations, fly back home and devote nine or ten months to business. Then, back to Europe and your leisurely explorations: Turkey, Israel, and Egypt. After visiting Cairo for a while, how about sailing up the Nile? Two or three months each summer exploring the perimeter of the Mediterranean would

still leave nine months or so each year for important work. That's a nice balance. Or, on your leisurely explorations, whenever you find a spot you especially like, just stay there as long as you like—spend the whole summer there if you like. No packing and unpacking, no fiddling with luggage and transfers. Just check in with customs at each new country. American dollars are welcome everywhere. And in your resting time, time spent on deck relaxing, you might want to get out the old yellow pad and make a few notes. Good ideas can be wooed anywhere. Just think—one idea you might get early one morning while sailing in the Adriatic Sea or the Aegean Sea could be worth millions when properly put to work back home. It might pay for the whole summer many times over. Remember, it isn't the time you spend working that matters as much as the good ideas you come up with and then put into operation. Besides, with nine months out of the year for productive effort, three months of leisure should produce dozens of excellent ideas. Ideas find leisure time the best soil in which to grow and show their bright, intriguing faces above ground. Taking three months off each year could be more productive than the traditional three weeks—more fun too! If you need to go back for any reason for a few days or a week, there are always airports nearby.

Let's say chartering the yacht costs two thousand dollars a week, including crew and cook, and you charter for twelve weeks. That's about twenty-five thousand dollars, plus extras, for the summer, plus airfare. Not bad. A lot cheaper than buying the yacht and having to maintain it and insure it year round. In fact, you could go on doing that for ten years or so and still save tons of money over what it would cost to buy and maintain your own boat. Besides, if you can't come up with the twenty-five-thousand-dollar idea in three months of floating around the Mediterranean, you're not thinking at all. Just don't forget to pack that yellow legal pad and a few good ballpoint pens. You might look for a yacht named *Eureka!* Surely somewhere in Greece…

Cruising around the Mediterranean could do wonders for your self-image. Who knows, you might find just the spot to build the loveliest little European-style American retirement village—with all European capital. Well, there's just no end to the good ideas that some leisurely world travel might engender. Wandering around small, offbeat villages, who knows what we might see or pick up in the way of an unusual product that might go over big back in the States?

And just for the hell of it, let's say that chartering the yacht costs twice twenty-five thousand dollars; that it costs you fifty thousand dollars a summer. You could still charter every summer for ten years and save money over what it would cost to own and maintain your own yacht.

There's only one good reason to own your own yacht, if that's what you would rather do. If owning your own yacht is important to you and you don't mind the annual hauling, scraping, and painting and the zillions of things that go wrong on a yacht and have to be repaired and the registration and the insurance and the rest of it, then by all means own your own yacht or your own airplane or RV or whatever. Because it's important that you do what you most want to do with the rewards you've earned from the service you've performed or provided. Besides, everybody needs his or her toy, and that's when what is practical has no place whatever in the picture. There are times to be impractical too.

I brought up the idea of cruising the coasts of the Mediterranean because I wanted to move your mind laterally, away from the ordinary. It's important that we think in new directions from time to time. The more often, the better. Genius has been defined as "the ability to think in new directions." After all, wasn't that what typified all the great geniuses you can think of? The great artists, composers, writers, inventors—they were all inventors, all creators, they all thought in new directions.

Life should be many things for all of us, but it should seldom, if ever, be boring. We don't have enough time to waste any of it in a state of boredom, or at least

any more than we have to. It may be necessary for us to attend meetings, but hopefully they can be kept as short and as close to the actual agenda as good manners permit. Even meetings can be made more interesting with a bit of preparation and originality.

In her marvelous book, *The Aquarian Conspiracy*, Marilyn Ferguson writes, "If we are not learning and teaching we are not awake and alive. Learning is not only like health, it is health."

One can be just as bored sitting in the cockpit of a yacht anchored in the harbor at Portofino as one can sitting in one's office in New York City at three o'clock on a Friday afternoon. But not if one is learning and teaching. Then boredom is never present. If you are at all like me, you require learning and teaching just about every day. I call it "doing some work," but learning and teaching are what it amounts to, in my case reading and writing (teaching). I need to know that I have done something worthwhile in order to fully enjoy my leisure time or a weekend. Perhaps that's the result of forty years of working, but for me there must be a balance of work and play—both to be fully enjoyed. I will never reach the age when I am no longer interested in learning or in putting what I have learned into language that others can understand, enjoy, and pass along. That seems to be my forte.

What are the odds that a person, following the guidelines of this program, will actually succeed? I would say his chances of failure are virtually nonexistent. The odds are overwhelmingly in one's favor; in fact, there's nothing else one can do but succeed! It's all in the goal and the planning that precede the establishment of that goal, if the person is a Goal Person. If the person is a River Person, he or she is automatically a success as long as he or she is swimming in that River.

It's like asking what the odds are that a person who has made up his or her mind to become a professional chef will actually become a professional chef. What else can that person become? Keep in mind that we're talking about people who are fully committed.

Remember the comment, "The American people can become anything they decide to become. The trouble is...they seldom make that decision."

I woke up one morning about fifteen minutes before the clock-radio alarm was to sound off. It was a great experience just to lie back and luxuriate. There popped into my mind the thought that life is its own reward. It came to me that having life itself—life being such a miraculous achievement—is like winning the grand prize. What we do after that—what we do with our lives—is the frosting on the cake.

We hear young people ask, "What is the purpose of life?" The purpose of life is service and whatever we decide to do or be to provide that service. We can do whatever we want with it. That is the terrible (to me, wonderful) freedom of the existentialists.

Never before have I been as conscious of how stunning an achievement life itself is, in all its forms. Perhaps that was how the great Dr. Albert Einstein felt about life and why he was so reverent about it in all its multifarious forms. We're so lucky to actually experience life, to be given the opportunity to do something worthwhile for others as our way of earning our way here, just as they spend their days serving us in so many ways. It becomes important then for us to do our work as creatively, as excellently as we can, and to think of new and better ways to do those things that it has been given us to do, so that we can maximize our input during the time we spend working.

I remember reading something about what an ongoing education will do for us. That it teaches us to love what doesn't cost much, to love the sunrise and the sunset and the beating of the rain on roof and windows and the gentle fall of snow on a winter day. The article went on to say that a good education teaches us to love life for its own sake. That's what I realized that morning when I woke up before the alarm sounded.

Being alive, just being alive, makes us winners. From then on, anything we want to add to the achievement is up to us. It needn't be a lot in the eyes of the world, but we can find our place in the scheme of things and do our thing––make our contribution whatever it happens to be.

One morning recently, Diana and I were in Hawaii. It was five o'clock and still pitch dark, but the sky was clear and filled with stars. We put on our bathing suits and walked out into the water until it was up to our shoulders. We put our arms around each other and drank in the clean warm breeze and luxuriated in the sea, now warm to our bodies. And as we watched, the sky in the east grew softly lighter until the great, craggy old volcanic mountains were clearly outlined against the early morning sky. What a joy it was—what a joy it is—just to be alive!

"If one advances confidently in the direction of his dreams, and endeavors to live the life he has imagined, he will meet with a success unexpected in common hours."

—HENRY DAVID THOREAU

ABOUT THE AUTHOR

EARL NIGHTINGALE could never have known that when he embarked on his journey to find the answers to the meaning of his life, that he would find a formula that would help millions of people around the world to find theirs as well.

Nightingale's messages of inspiration were for the most part audio, but found their beginnings when written on the pages of legal yellow pads, and while he was hailed for his audio programs and radio shows, he waited a lifetime before fulfilling his desire to write a book. When he wrote *Earl Nightingale's Greatest Discovery*, it was recognized and rewarded when the Napoleon Hill Foundation presented Earl with a Gold Medal for Literary Excellence.

The story about Sparky that he tells in this book has been licensed many times for use in educational teaching books and serves as inspiration for those young people who have been told repeatedly that they are "losers."

More than sixty years have passed since Nightingale wrote and recorded *The Strangest Secret*, and his works and messages have stood the test of time and still sell, daily, around the world.

Earl Nightingale is recognized as the greatest philosopher of his century. He was invited to the White House by the president, invited to visit and meet Queen Elizabeth, and received the keys to cities around the world. Earl Nightingale sat at the tables of dignitaries at home and abroad.

Among his numerous awards, he treasured most those presented by the following organizations:

- Columbia Records—Gold Record for *The Strangest Secret*
- Toastmasters International—Golden Gavel Award
- National Speakers Association
- His induction into the National Association of Broadcasters, Radio Hall of Fame

Earl Nightingale passed away on March 25, 1989.

The book *Learning to Fly As a Nightingale* was written by his widow, Diana Nightingale, and tells of their individual lives before meeting each other, their time together, and Diana finding the courage to go on after her husband's death.

In her book, where she shares a side of Earl Nightingale few have ever seen, you will get to know Earl Nightingale, the man, the storyteller, and the dreamer.

EARL NIGHTINGALE
WALL OF AWARDS

Earl and Diana with Leo Buscaglia

Napoleon Hill Gold Medal Award

One of many honorary degrees

National Association of Broadcasters
Earl Nightingale & Red Motley

After speaking at Carnegie Hall

Guests of the Governor of Guam

Nightingale with Her Majesty, Elizabeth, Queen of England.

Toastmasters International

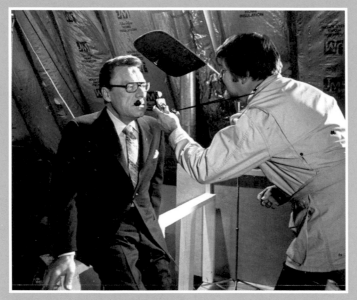

Television Days

Lowell Thomas and Earl Nightingale

Earl and Diana Nightingale

"We Become What We Think About."
(Earl Nightingale, 1921- 1989)

NEW! Only from Simple Truths®

IGNITE READS
spark impact in just one hour

IGNITE READS IS A NEW SERIES OF 1-HOUR READS WRITTEN BY WORLD-RENOWNED EXPERTS!

These captivating books will help you become the best version of yourself, allowing for new opportunities in your personal and professional life. Accelerate your career and expand your knowledge with these powerful books written on today's hottest ideas.

TRENDING BUSINESS AND PERSONAL GROWTH TOPICS

Read in an hour or less

Leading experts and authors

Bold design and captivating content